Paws
AND
Claws

WOLVES

Sara Swan Miller

PowerKiDS press.

New York

For Jaik and Boogie,
your friends and relations

Published in 2008 by The Rosen Publishing Group, Inc.
29 East 21st Street, New York, NY 10010

First Edition

Editor: Amelie von Zumbusch
Book Design: Julio Gil
Photo Researcher: Nicole Pristash

Photo Credits: Cover, pp. 5, 7, 9, 13, 21 Shutterstock.com; p. 11 © istockphoto.com/Chris Crafter; p. 15 © SuperStock, Inc.; pp. 17, 19 © istockphoto.com/John Pitcher.

Library of Congress Cataloging-in-Publication Data

Miller, Sara Swan.
  Wolves / Sara Swan Miller. — 1st ed.
      p. cm. — (Paws and claws)
  Includes index.
  ISBN 978-1-4042-4161-9 (library binding)
  1. Wolves—Juvenile literature. I. Title.
  QL737.C22M553 2008
  599.773—dc22
                                              2007018164

Manufactured in the United States of America

Contents

What Is a Wolf?

Look at this picture of a gray wolf. Doesn't it look like a large dog? There is a good reason for that. Wolves and dogs are part of the same family. That family also includes **coyotes** and foxes. Wolves once lived all over the world. The only places they have never lived are Australia and Antarctica.

Today there are just three **species**, or types, of wolves. These are the gray wolf, the red wolf, and the Ethiopian wolf. All wolves are great hunters. They can bring down animals much larger than themselves, including **caribou** and **moose**.

Gray wolves, like this wolf, are also known as timber wolves.
"Timber" means "wood."

Beautiful and Strong

Wolves have very warm, thick fur. Their fur is generally gray or black, although some wolves are reddish. Wolves that live in the Arctic have white fur.

Wolves have very strong jaws, or mouths. Their teeth are huge and very sharp. Their strong jaws and teeth help make wolves such good hunters. Wolves also have excellent eyesight and very good hearing. Their pointed ears can pick up the sounds of other animals from far away. However, a wolf's big nose is its most important tool for finding food. A wolf's sense of smell is about 100 times better than ours!

Baby wolves generally have blue eyes. However, most wolves' eyes turn yellow, brown, or orange when they grow up.

Powerful Paws

Wolves have long, strong legs. They can run as fast as 35 miles per hour (56 km/h). Wolves can cover up to 30 miles (48 km) a night.

Wolves have huge paws and sharp claws that help them **grip** the ground. Wolves do not use their claws to catch their **prey**, however. They use their teeth for that. Wolves have five toes on their front paws. One of these toes, called a dewclaw, is not needed. It is up on the inside of the wolf's leg and never touches the ground. Wolves have just four toes on their back paws.

Dewclaws

Some pet dogs have dewclaws on all four feet. However, wolves have dewclaws only on their front feet.

Wolf Packs

Wolves live together in family groups, called packs. There are generally six to eight wolves in a pack, but packs may have more than 30 wolves.

The leaders of the pack are called the alpha male and the alpha female. They generally stay together all their life and **mate** only with each other. The alpha pair is the mother and father of the pack's pups. The other wolves in the pack are most often the pups' older brothers and sisters. Some packs have wolves called the beta male and beta female. They are the most important wolves after the alpha pair.

Wolf packs work together to find food and to care for the pack's pups.

Their Own Territory

Each wolf pack lives in its own special area, called its **territory**. If there is plenty of prey to eat, the pack's territory may be only 30 square miles (78 sq km). Where there are not many animals to hunt, a pack's territory may be as big as 800 square miles (2,072 sq km).

Wolves mark their territory with scent. The alpha male sprays **urine** on trees and rocks around the territory's edge. This tells other wolves, "Go away! This is ours!" If a strange wolf dares to enter its territory, the wolf pack will drive it away.

Wolf packs that hunt big animals, such as moose, or animals that move with the seasons, such as caribou, generally have the largest territory.

The Hunt

When it is time for the pack to hunt, the wolves start **howling** loudly. Howling together gets the pack ready for the job ahead. They set forth quietly, smelling the air. When the wolves spot their prey, they run up from behind. They bite at the animal's backside to weaken it. Finally, they catch it by the nose or throat and bring it down.

After the kill, the wolves set about eating up all the meat. A wolf has a very large stomach. It can eat 20 pounds (9 kg) of meat at a time.

Because wolves eat so much meat at one time, they can go several days before they eat again.

Wolf Pups

Wolf pups are born in the spring. First their mother digs a den. The pups will be safe there. Mothers generally have four to seven pups at a time. Wolf pups weigh only 1 pound (.5 kg) when they are born. Pups are weak and cannot see or hear. For the first three weeks, they live on their mother's milk.

As the pups grow older, the pack's other wolves begin bringing the pups meat. They carry it to the den in their stomach, already chewed. The pups lick an older wolf's mouth to get it to throw up the meat.

Wolf pups begin to see when they are about two weeks old.
Pups start to hear at three weeks old.

Growing Up

About three weeks after they are born, wolf pups come out of the den for the first time. They play games, chasing and jumping on each other. They also jump on bugs and other small animals. Play fighting and play hunting gets the pups ready for real hunting.

Two months after they are born, pups leave the den for good. While the rest of the pack hunts, the pups wait at a **rendezvous site**. The other wolves will meet and feed them there. By the fall, the pups are grown and ready to hunt with the rest of the pack.

The rendezvous sites where pups wait are generally grassy places in a forest clearing or on the edge of a forest.

Wolves in Trouble

The wolves of the world are having a hard time. There are far fewer wolves today than there were a few hundred years ago. For example, gray wolves used to be found in forests all over North America. Long ago, there were about 2,000,000 of them. Now there are fewer than 100,000.

People are the wolves' main problem. For centuries, people have hunted and poisoned wolves. People did this because they feared that wolves would eat their sheep and cows, or even kill people. People also cut down the wolves' forest homes. They built towns where wolves used to live.

Red wolves, like this wolf, are the least common kind of wolf. Today, there are only a few hundred red wolves.

Helping Wolves

Luckily, some people are helping wolves make a comeback. These people know that wolves keep the herds they hunt healthy. Wolves often eat weak or sick animals. This keeps herds from growing too big. Big herds often cannot find enough food to eat.

One way people help wolves is by bringing them back to places where they once lived. In 1995, 14 gray wolves from Canada were brought to live in Yellowstone Park. The wolves mated, had pups, and formed several packs. Today, Yellowstone has about 300 gray wolves! This gives us hope that wolves will be around for years to come.

Glossary

caribou (KER-eh-boo) Large deer that live in the North American Arctic.

coyotes (ky-OH-teez) Animals that live in North America and look like small, thin wolves.

grip (GRIP) To hold something firmly.

howling (HOW-ling) Making a loud, long cry.

mate (MAYT) To come together to make babies.

moose (MOOS) A large, heavy kind of deer.

prey (PRAY) An animal that is hunted by another animal for food.

rendezvous site (RON-dih-voo SYT) The place wolf pups stay while the rest of their pack is hunting.

species (SPEE-sheez) One kind of living thing. All people are one species.

territory (TER-uh-tor-ee) Land or space that animals guard for their use.

urine (YUR-un) A liquid waste made by the body.

Index

A
Antarctica, 4
Arctic, 6
Australia, 4

C
caribou, 4
coyotes, 4

D
dog, 4

E
ears, 6
eyesight, 6

F
family, 4
foxes, 4
fur, 6

G
ground, 8

H
hearing, 6
hunters, 4, 6

J
jaws, 6

M
moose, 4
mouth(s), 6, 16

P
pack(s), 10, 12, 14, 18, 22
prey, 8, 12, 14

S
species, 4

T
teeth, 6, 8

Web Sites

Due to the changing nature of Internet links, PowerKids Press has developed an online list of Web sites related to the subject of this book. This site is updated regularly. Please use this link to access the list:
www.powerkidslinks.com/paws/wolves/